THE CIRCULATION OF THE BLOOD

BY STEWART ROSS

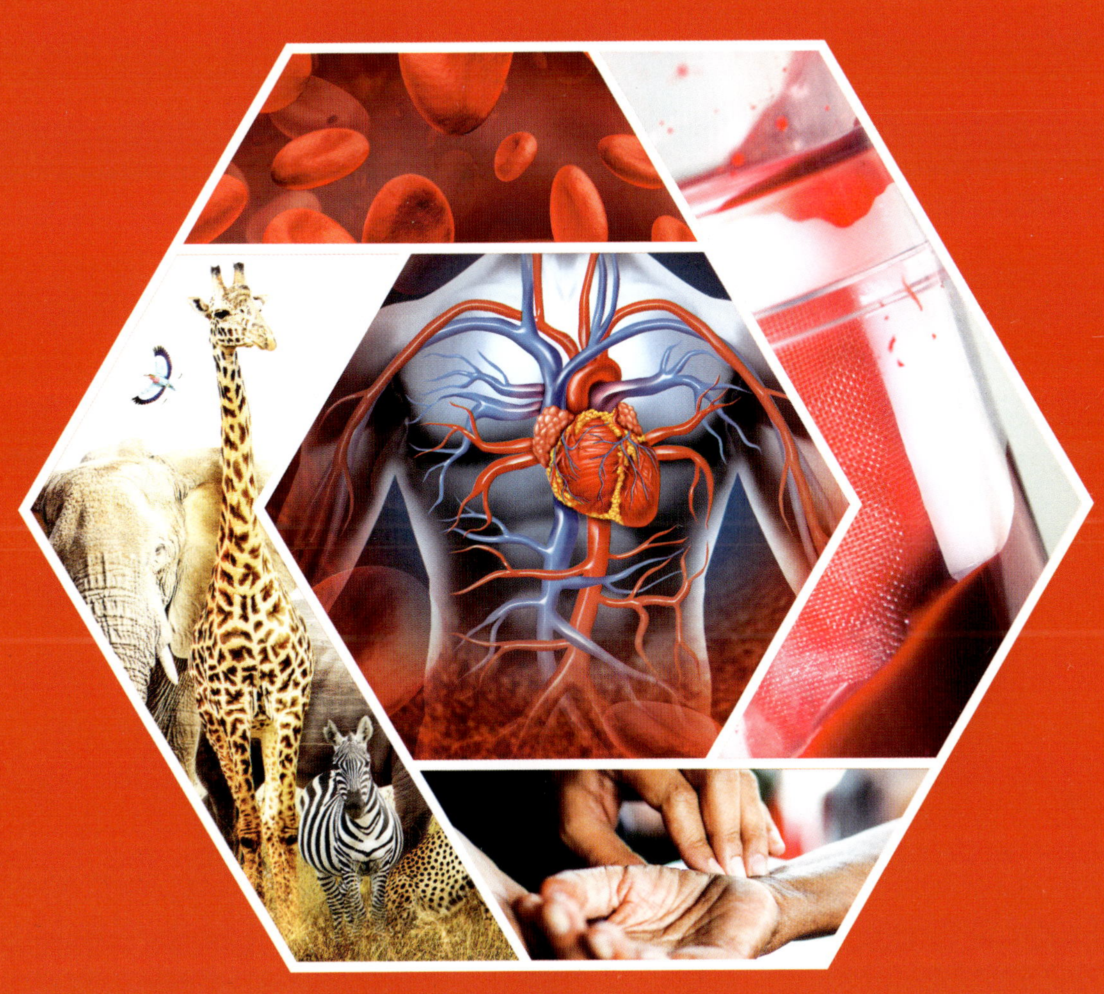

Text by Stewart Ross in cooperation with Christine Clover.
© copyright in this edition Tulip Books 2019

The right of the Author to be identified as the Author of this work
has been asserted by the Author in accordance with the Copyright,
Designs and Patents Act 1988.

Every attempt has been made by the Publisher to secure appropriate
permissions for material reproduced in this book. If there has been any
oversight we will be happy to rectify the situation in future editions or
reprints. Written submissions should be made to the Publishers.

ISBN 978-1-78388-147-5

Index

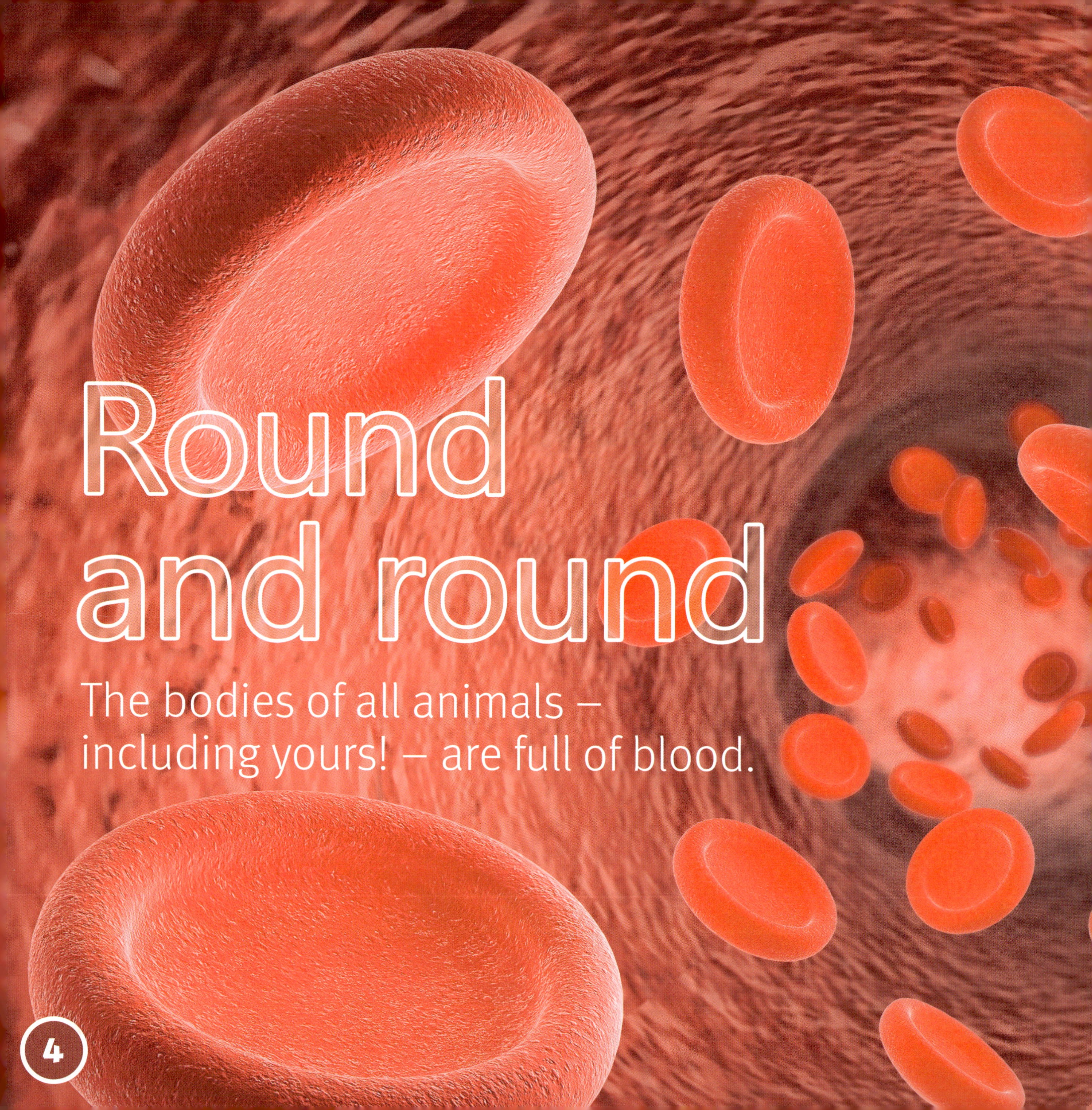

Round
and round

The bodies of all animals —
including yours! — are full of blood.

4

It is pumped in tubes, called *veins*
and *arteries*, round and round the body.

This is called the circulation of the blood.

5

The invisible gas

To live, we need oxygen.
This is an invisible gas in the air.
We take in oxygen when we
breathe air into our **lungs**.

Blood carries oxygen round
the body, to our brain and
muscles.

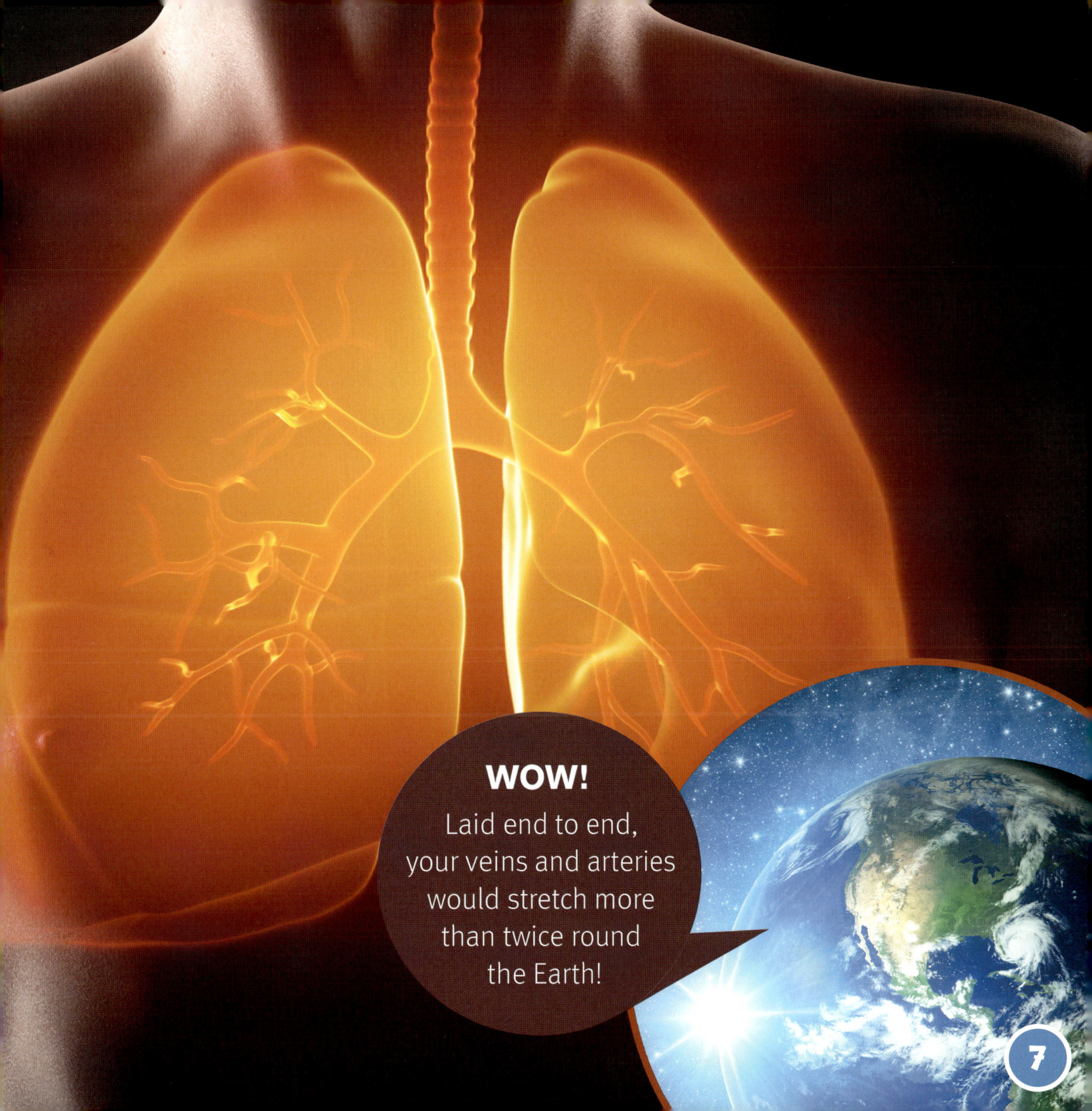

WOW!
Laid end to end, your veins and arteries would stretch more than twice round the Earth!

The heart pump

The heart is a pump.
It pumps blood out through *arteries*.
It returns to the heart through *veins*.

It you look at your wrists,
you'll see blue lines.
These are veins.

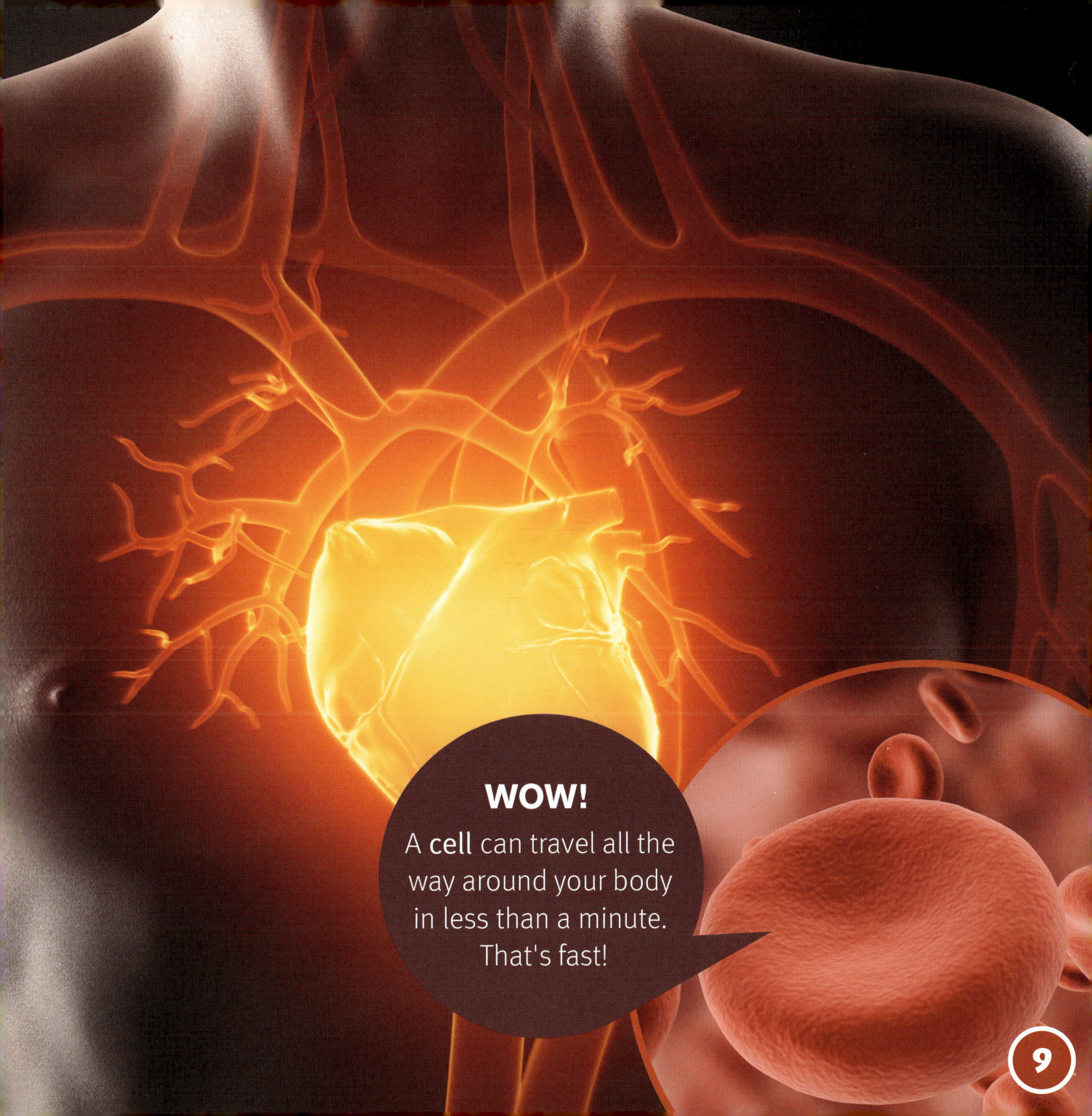

WOW!
A cell can travel all the way around your body in less than a minute. That's fast!

Slow start

It took thousands of years to learn that blood circulated.

The ancient Egyptians believed the heart was joined to 46 tubes, called 'channels'.

These included the veins, lungs and **intestines**.

The Egyptians didn't know these **organs** had different jobs.

Galen gets it wrong

Galen was an important Roman doctor.
He **researched** the blood by **dissecting** animals.
But he got some things wrong.

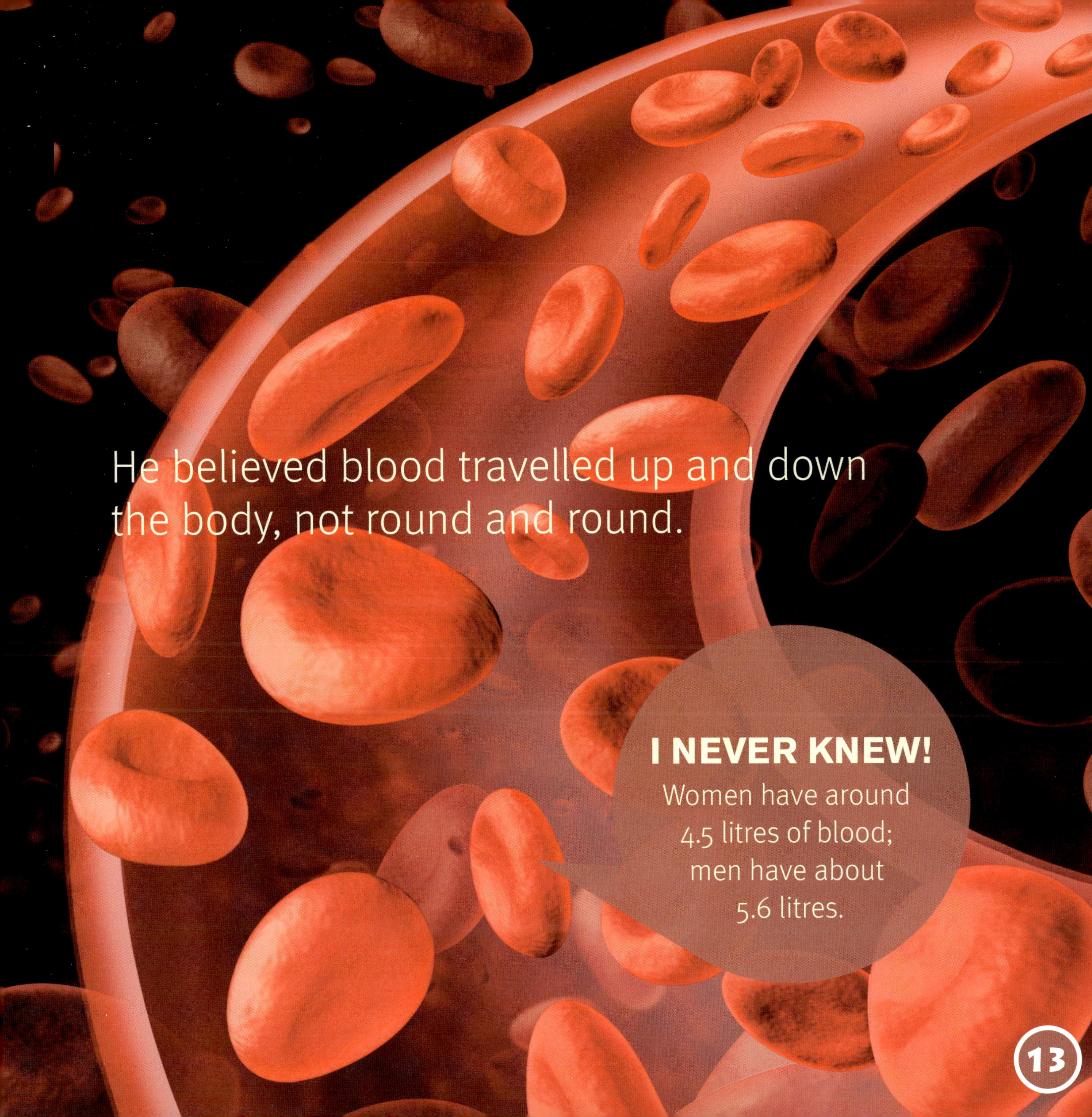

He believed blood travelled up and down the body, not round and round.

I NEVER KNEW!
Women have around 4.5 litres of blood; men have about 5.6 litres.

13

Ibn al-Nafis

The Arab scholar Ibn al-Nafis (born 1213) **discovered** that the heart is a pump. He saw that blood circulated in and out of the heart and lungs.

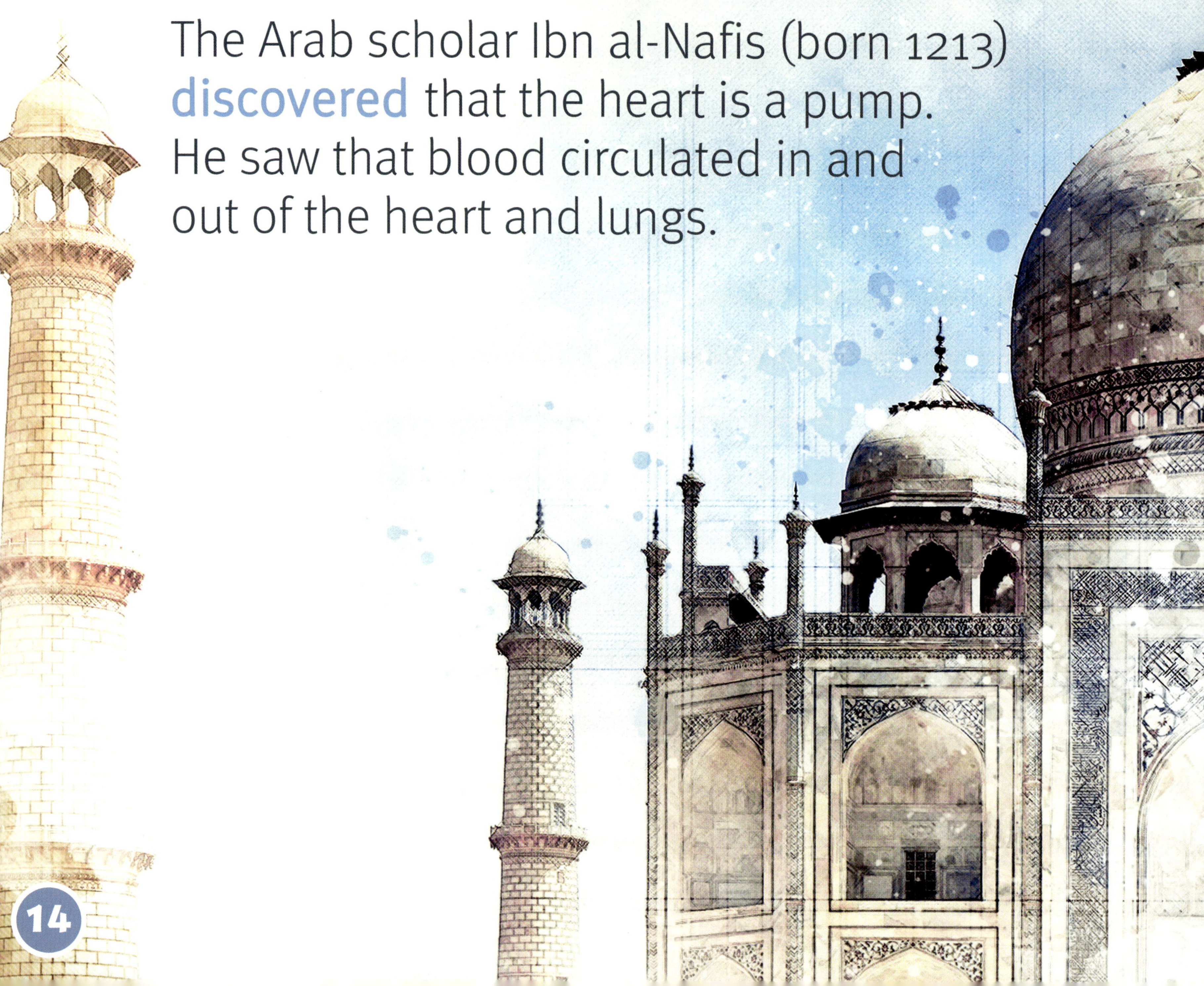

But he did not realise
it went right round the body.

William Harvey

William Harvey (born 1578) was the first person to describe the circulation of the blood in detail.

He showed how the heart pumped blood to the lungs, the brain and the rest of the body.

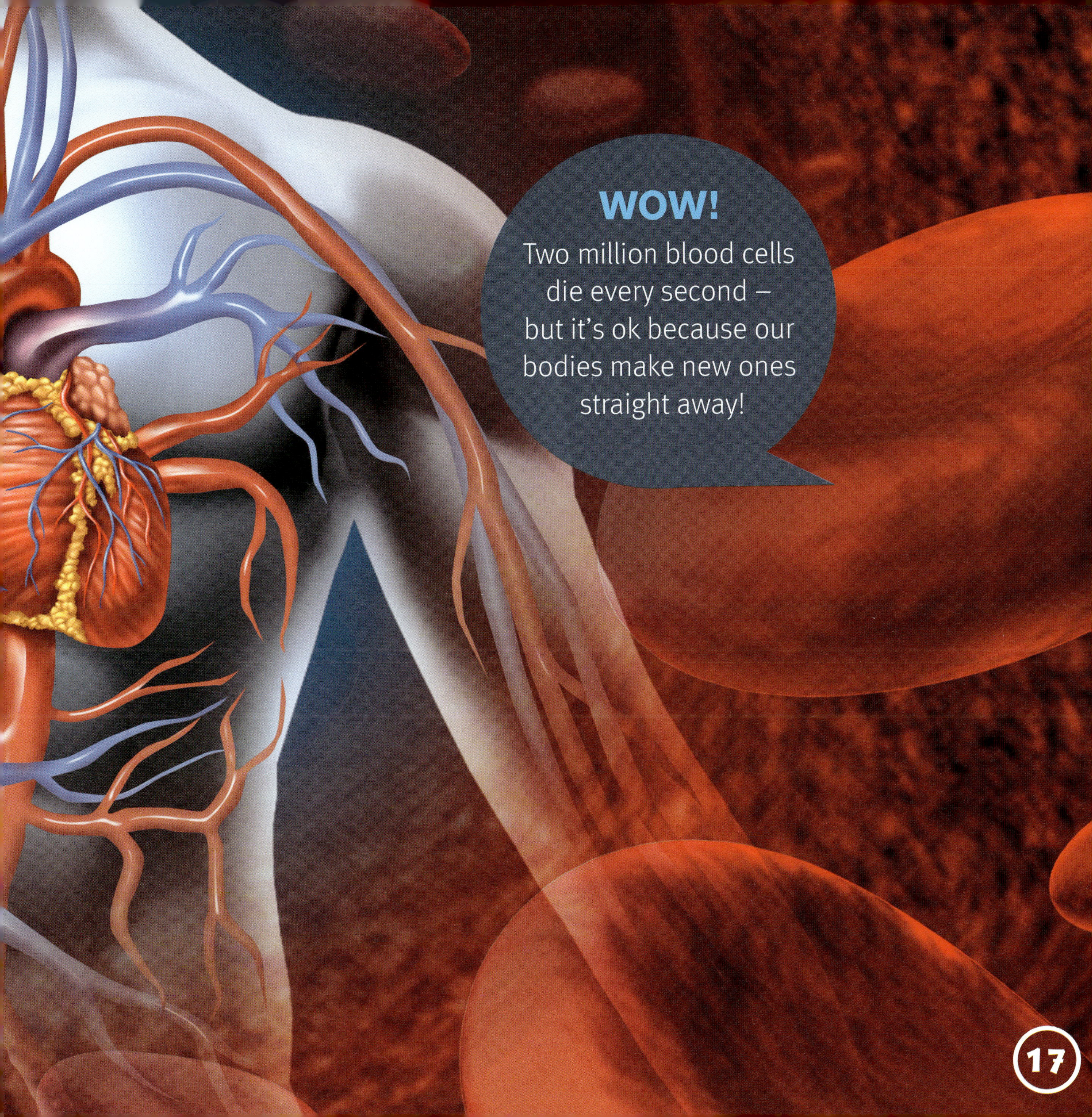

WOW!
Two million blood cells die every second – but it's ok because our bodies make new ones straight away!
17

Mini tubes

Harvey knew blood went out in arteries and back in veins.But what happened in between?

Marcello Malpighi (born 1628) found the answer with his **microscope**: it went through mini tubes called *capillaries*.

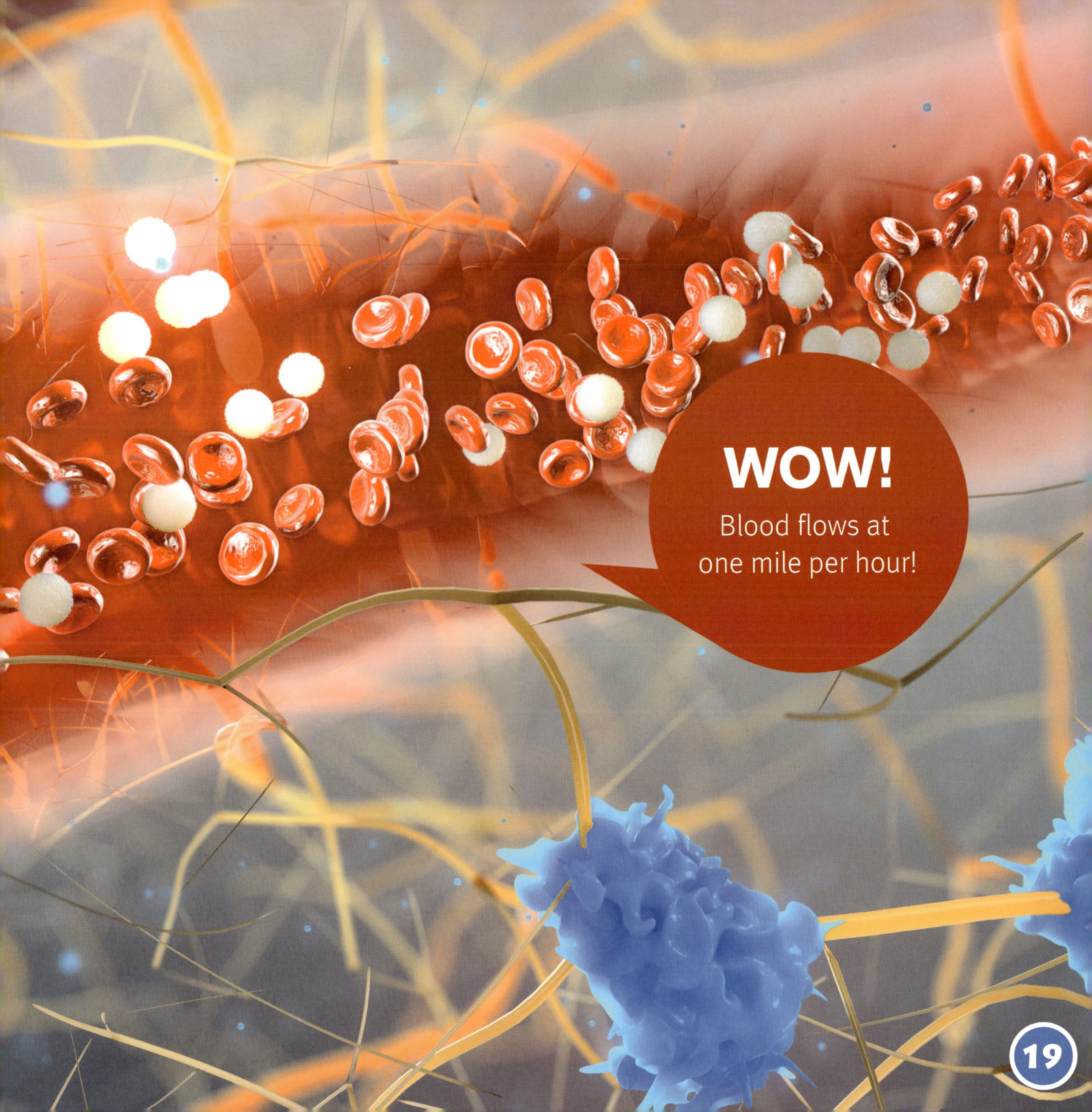
WOW!
Blood flows at
one mile per hour!
19

Using science

After Ibn al-Nafis,
Harvey and Malpighi,
scientists learned masses
more about the blood.
Doctors used this research
to treat patients.

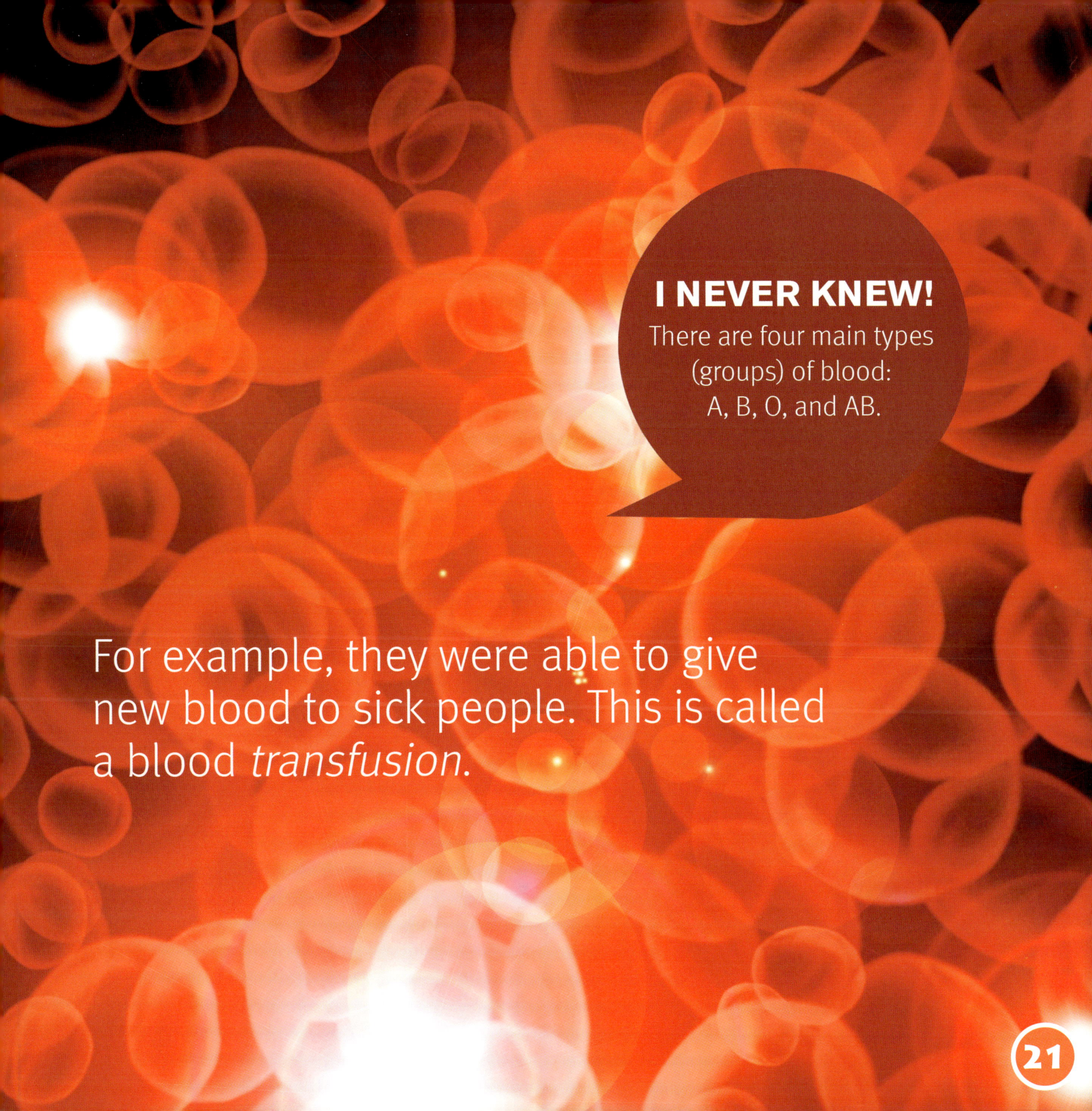

I NEVER KNEW!
There are four main types (groups) of blood: A, B, O, and AB.

For example, they were able to give new blood to sick people. This is called a blood *transfusion*.

21

Heart swap

Doctors can now give a sick patient
a new heart! This is called a heart *transplant*.
It is a long and difficult **operation**.

The new heart has to come
from someone who has recently died.

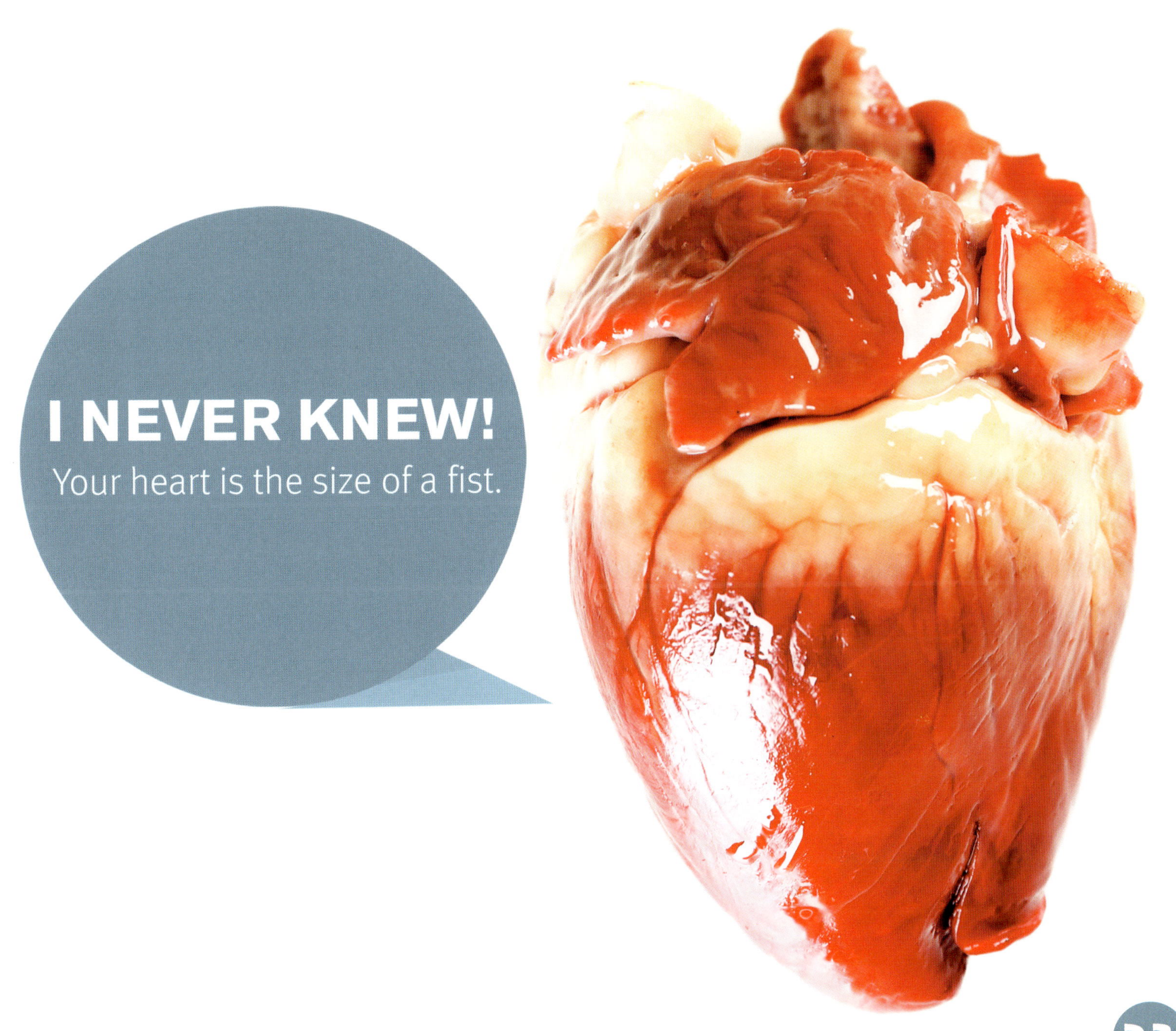

Glossary

Cell
Tiny part of every living thing.

Discover
Find out for the first time.

Dissect
Cutting up a plant or dead animal to study it.

Intestines
The insides or 'guts' of an animal. The intestines digest food.

Lungs
Part of the body (in the chest) that takes oxygen from the air
and passes it into the blood. We have two longs, left and right.

Microscope
A magnifying machine for examining things that the eye cannot see.

Operation
Cutting into a body to cure an injury or illness.

Organ
Part of the insides of an animal with an important job to do.

Research
Examining a subject carefully to find out more about it.